The Undying Faith Book 5. A Guide to a Life of Success and Happiness

The undying faith., Volume 5

Hebert McQuinn

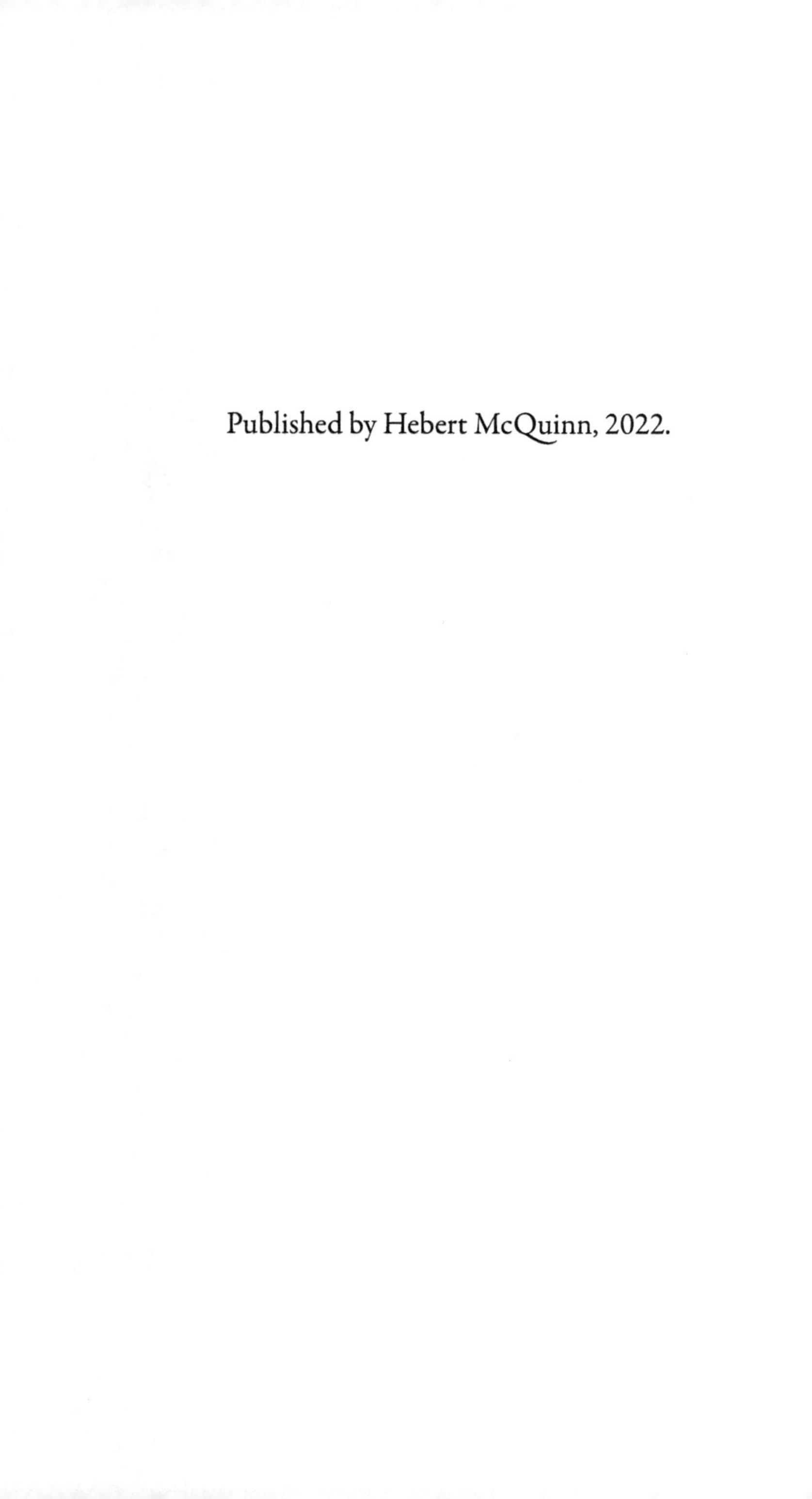

Published by Hebert McQuinn, 2022.

While every precaution has been taken in the preparation of this book, the publisher assumes no responsibility for errors or omissions, or for damages resulting from the use of the information contained herein.

THE UNDYING FAITH BOOK 5. A GUIDE TO A LIFE OF SUCCESS AND HAPPINESS

First edition. August 17, 2022.

Copyright © 2022 Hebert McQuinn.

ISBN: 979-8215962107

Written by Hebert McQuinn.

Table of Contents

To Nonhlanhla Pretty Zwane, for being this amazing inspiration in my life.

Foreword

This book is the fifth in a series of five books. The author trusts that the preceeding four have had the intended effect of inspiring and hopefully educating the reader on the topics tackled therein.

The author hopes with this installment to plug the gaps left by the foregoing books, as well as provide a recap of some of the topics discussed in the preceeding four books.

The author also trusts that the journey from Book 1 up to this point has been one wherein some value has been derived by the reader from the interaction with the literary works.

This particular book is for the author like an arrival after a long journey which has been an enjoyable as well as a spiritually enriching experience. It is for this reason a special book for the author and hopefully it will be for the reader too.

The idea of writing the books was inspired by the result of the author's search for the truth about Jesus Christ and the Bible as the Christian doctrine. The author has in his search uncovered what he believes is the truth he has been searching for and his immediate instinct was to want to share it with as many people as possible and to spread the message far and wide.

It is hard to come across such valuable information and not share. As the great American poetess Maya Angelou once said:

"Those who learn, must teach." It is the author's hope that that does not make him come across as arrogant in any way. It's just that he believes that the value of the truth is in its utility and sharing.

The Bible and all its contents is humanity's common heritage and the author believes that it was written with the purpose to equip humanity with knowledge of the truth about things mental, emotional and spiritual. Please join the author and engage in the further elucidation of these matters in the pages that follow.

The series is written mindful of the fact that success means different things to different people so the author has tried to make the underlying principles all encompassing and applicable no matter what the reader's definition of success is. The principles underpinning success are essentially the same. Do not only read but also apply the principles and internalize the lessons learned. The value of the principles and lessons in this series of books is in their utility.

Otherwise if we hear and not do the word we've looked ourselves in the mirror, walked away and completely forgot what we looked like. By reading, learning and applying what you have learned you will derive the most value from the series. Passive reading can only provide entertainment at the most and no additional value to the reader. With that said, the author invites you to now engage with this, the final book in this magnanimous series. Enjoy and be inspired.

Hebert McQuinn: Author

Chapter 1
The workings of faith

I know that I have dedicated a chapter to and wrote at length on the topic of faith in a previous book. But due to the importance of the topic, I felt that I had to do a recap on it. Please allow me. The Bible tells us that Jesus, the son of God was a powerful man who did a lot of wondrous works and performed many miracles. We are told that he did all these things for the glory of God, so that people would believe that he is the son of God and believe in him and God his father.

But I will cite examples from the Bible that give us insight into his performance of miracles. In Luke 8:48 we read the following: *"And he said unto her, Daughter, be of good comfort; thy faith hath made thee whole; go in peace."* A woman who, having had an issue of blood for twelve years, and who had spent all her money on physicians with no healing decided one day to come behind Jesus when he was surrounded by a crowd of people, and touch the border of his garment, believing that having done so, she would be healed of her illness. And having on the day, actually touched the border of his garment, her issue of blood stanched immediately, we are told.

Jesus felt her touch because it was no ordinary touch, he said he felt it because he had perceived that virtue had gone out of him, as a result of that touch. It is important to note that Jesus had not actively done anything to the woman. She was the one who acted in touching the border of his garment. She did that because she believed that she would be healed of her illness after having touched the border of his garment.

Jesus wanted to know who touched him, to the surprise of his disciples as he was surrounded by a crowd and there were many who were touching him. After he had explained the effect that this particular touch had on him, the woman came forward and explained what had happened. Jesus, having learned what had happened, did not say that his power had healed the woman's illness. Instead he tells her that her faith had made her well. Her faith, not Jesus's power, her faith was responsible for the miraculous healing that happened to her.

In Luke 17: 19 we read: *"And he said unto him, Arise, go thy way: thy faith hat made thee whole."* These are the words that we are told that Jesus uttered to the leper who returned to thank him for his healing. There were ten of them, the lepers that Jesus told to go and show themselves to the priests. We are told that as they went, they were healed. Now, the practice for lepers in those days was for them to live in self isolation until they were healed and to show themselves to the priests when they were healed.

So when Jesus told them to go and show themselves to the priests they were to assume and believe that they were already healed from that point onwards. Following Jesus's orders they believed that by the time they presented themselves to the priests they would be completely healed and it happened as they believed, on their way to the priests they were healed, and one of them returned to thank Jesus. But once again Jesus did not take the credit for having healed a sick person. He told him that his faith had made him well.

In Luke 18:42 we read the following: "*And Jesus said unto him, Receive thy sight; thy faith hath saved thee.*" That is what Jesus said to the blind man who screamed to him and wouldn't be silenced in his request for Jesus to heal him of his blindness. It would seem that the more they sought to silence him, the louder he shouted. Jesus heard him, came to him, gave him back his sight and told him that his faith has saved him.

Nowhere had Jesus taken credit for healing a person. He did whatever he did or said whatever he said to the sick person and would invariably say afterwards that the person's faith was responsible for the actual healing. Jesus did not want us to lack knowledge of the real power behind his great works. He taught us that they were made possible by the faith of the afflicted, and not by his personal might.

As Jesus was moving from place to place teaching and performing many miracles, it so happened that one day he found himself in his hometown of Galilee on his usual mission of spreading the word of God. In Mark 6:5-6 we read: "*And he could there do no mighty work, save that he laid his hands upon a few sick folk and healed them {6:6} And he marveled because of their unbelief. And he went round the villages, teaching.*"

For Jesus to do mighty work, he depended on the faith of the people in the community where he was working. This truth was nowhere as clearly illustrated as it was in the town of Galilee where people were in effect claiming that he was a charlatan. They claimed to know that he was the son of Joseph the carpenter and they knew his brothers and sisters. They simply didn't buy into the narrative of him being the Messiah and son of God.

The Bible says that he could do no mighty work there, absolutely no mighty work. And it was because of the unbelief of the residents of the town. In the absence of faith, even the son of God cannot do much. For mighty work to be possible, the precondition of belief is necessary. That is just how powerful the concepts of belief and faith are. Without faith we cannot effect the self transformation we need to raise ourselves to a higher state of consciousness in order for us to have and be what we want to have and be.

Chapter 2

The unlimited resources at your disposal

When you have prayed for something and you have believed when you were praying that you have received what you were praying for, and you have maintained that belief beyond the point of prayer, your feelings of joy and gratitude will make an impression on the Subconscious mind. If you have read the other books in the series you will know that the Subconscious mind, once impressed with the feelings, will immediately start to mobilize everything and every person that needs to play a role in the manifestation of the desired thing in the corporeal world.

For this to happen you will be able to do what you need to do to attract the resources that you need to fulfill your desire. I know this may seem like mumbo-jumbo but things will happen just the way they should and one thing will lead to another till the desired thing is objectified in the physical world, once the Subconscious mind has been sufficiently impressed with the feelings of possession and gratitude. If you believe that the resources required for the realization of the desire do exist and are limitless, you will be able to recognize them as they appear to you and you will be able to utilize them in edging closer to the complete fulfillment of your desire.

If at anytime in the process you need to learn a new skill, a teacher will appear. You will find the appropriate course and the right teacher and mentor. If you need money to register for the course you will find ways and means to obtain the finance required for registration. All that you need to do is believe that the resources at your disposal are unlimited. This way you get yourself into a mindset of abundance. Things can only be scarce to you if you believe that resources are hard to find because there is not enough of them for everyone, or that they are just generally hard to come by. Things happen to you according to your belief.

When you keep in mind the belief in ownership of the thing desired, you are attracting into your world, through the medium of your Subconscious mind all that is required for its manifestation in the corporeal world. I believe in this principle because I have recent living experience of its workings. I have always known that at some point in my life I would write a book, and some time in November of 2021 the idea occurred to me that the time has come for me to finally write that book.

I knew what I wanted to write about but I knew nothing about writing books or what the requirements were for being a published author. How books get printed and end up in bookstores I did not know. But I had a book idea and I believed that I could just surprise myself and everyone by actually writing and publishing a book and have it sold in famous bookstores the world over. The thing is I just didn't know where to start. But I had already an image of myself as a published author, I could feel what it was like to be a published author.

And then one day as I was going through my emails, an advert for a book writing and publishing course caught my eye. I immediately clicked on it and read the content. When I was done reading I was more and more convinced that I could have the answer to my prayer by registering for the course, which I did without much ado. When they emailed me the course content I realized it was a lengthy course and a very tricky one for an absolute beginner and after my initial engagement with it I had a lot of questions about its contents racing through my mind.

There didn't seem to be any customer support associated with the course and I found that disappointing. I didn't even know how or where I would do my writing when eventually I would get around to doing it. And then one day a thought occurred to me that I could use my android phone to write my book. I immediately acted on that thought and just began writing and I finished one page, two pages, three pages. Then I started to believe that I could actually pull it off and write a 25 page A4 size book on the subject I had chosen. It took me two weeks to write and finish the book.

In the meantime the course presenter had reached out to me with follow-up emails in which he was explaining the course content and advising on how best to approach it. I had my manuscript written already and I went back into the course to learn how to publish it. That is when I learned about Amazon's Kindle Direct Publishing and how to publish your book on the online platform. On the platform I learned about how to format a manuscript for publishing. I learned all about book covers.

The long and the short of it is I have had my trials and errors in book publishing but the resources I needed to make headway always appeared when I needed them, as if by magic, because

I believed that I would find all the resources that I needed to become a published author. And naively I believed that that was all I needed to do to reach readers and sell a lot of books. Two months later I checked out the stats on KDP and realized to my dismay that I hadn't had a single book sold to date. That worried me but I knew that there were resources available to me that I could use to get to the bottom of this problem and find a solution.

I found out that there was a thing called book marketing and promotion that I had to learn and do. The resources I needed to realize this just appeared to me as and when I needed them. I met the people that I needed to meet and, looking back I must admit that was relatively easy for me to get to the point where I was satisfied that I knew all that I needed to know about that part of being an author. I came across and was able to purchase the necessary software and I must admit everything just went smoothly because I had access to all the resources. In addition I had the time and money. I was never short of anything.

When the writers of the Bible tell us to believe that we receive what we are praying for when we pray, they want us to have a mindset of abundance. When we start believing we don't have any doubt as to whether we have the resources necessary for fulfillment of our desire or not. We don't entertain thoughts about what shortages there may be in resources that could make the fulfillment of our desire impossible. We are to believe that whatever needs to happen for us to realize our dream will happen. We don't involve ourselves with what ifs, we just know that somehow it will happen for us and a way will be made. We don't make excuses like " I don't have money " or "I don't have the time ". We just believe that we will have whatever we need to realize our desire.

Always believe in a present and future wherein it is possible to do and be whatever you want to do and be. Believing that we have what we were praying for or believing that we are already what we wanted to be when we prayed brings the law of reversibility into play. It will be as though a stairway is lowered for you to climb towards the physical counterpart of your desire and all that you have to do is climb, one rung after another. Once your feelings of elation and possession are impressed upon the Subconscious mind, the steps you need to take towards the realization of your desire will become recognizable to you and all that will remain is for you to take action.

In as much as the foregoing may seem like an easy way to achieve success, which it is believe me, it doesn't take away the need to take your physical and mental capabilities into account when deciding on what you want to achieve. With all of the above in mind, there is still a need for you to set realistic goals for yourself.

Everyone has things that they can find which they would love doing, when you have found something which you think you would love doing, the doing becomes easy if you have the aptitude as well. When you have found something that you love doing you are not easily dissuaded or discouraged. Your enjoyment of your daily tasks will make you go the extra mile each time resulting in you achieving your goal in record time.

When thinking about something to do to improve your life conditions and change your circumstance, always go for something that you will enjoy doing, a goal that means the world to you, and then pray for success in making it a reality. Feel like you would feel had you already done it successfully. Daily imagine yourself having done it successfully and be on the lookout for steps to take in pursuit of your goal. You need to have enough confidence in yourself to believe that you are capable of successfully performing all the tasks required to be performed in order to realize your goal.

You have to be realistic about the skills and expertise that you possess and those that you will be required to acquire in pursuit of your goal. In your areas of inadequacy find resources by the use of which you can learn and acquire the skills and expertise. As long as you remain focused on your goal the resources you will need at every step will appear. Your Subconscious will make them available because the law of reversibility and the law of attraction will have come into play.

Chapter 3
What you are really worth.

A person's real worth is very important in determining what is due to them, what they deserve to be getting in the vocation of their choice. There are many people who are being shortchanged where they work and many who actually shortchange themselves, because they don't know what they are really worth.

Whatever you do in your line of work should add some kind of value to the product or service of your company or should satisfy the needs of your clients in a way that no other product or service can. Your real worth will be in proportion to the usefulness of your product or service.

You have to periodically take inventory of your skills and expertise because they are your main assets, when everything is taken away from you as it happens in life sometimes, that is what you will remain with. That is why you have to learn to optimize the utility of your skills and expertise for the greatest returns. When you know your real worth you know what you are bringing to the table when negotiating contracts of work in whatever form.

Now there are people who are content, for whatever reason, to stay in one occupation for many years till it's time for them to retire. One of the reasons they do this is because they enjoy what they are doing and wouldn't trade it for anything in the world. Well, good for them, in a way I think they are a lucky bunch because there are some people who go through life without ever finding any kind of work that they can be good at and actually enjoy doing. People in the latter category are really unfortunate in my opinion. The other reason people stay in one occupation for a lifetime is fear of change or fear of failing at a new venture and therefore choosing to stick with what you know.

People even stay in jobs that they don't like because of the reasons above. They would wake up every morning with a heavy heart and wish they didn't have to go. Well there are a lot of varied reasons why a person would hate the job they have. A boss from hell, co-workers from hell, physically, mentally or emotionally draining work etcetera. Whatever your reason it is just not worth staying in a job you hate because if you do that you are living in contradiction to your character and it can be extremely damaging to you psychologically. The emotional stress that comes with doing work that you hate or working in an environment that you hate becomes a permanent feature of your life, together with all the illnesses normally related to a stressful life and the attendant loss of the sense of self-worth.

You have to make a change before you reach the breaking point or before the breaking point takes you down a dark abyss from which there will be no easy way to escape. You have to remind yourself If you find yourself in this kind of situation that you are a child of God and that He created you to be able to enjoy life and be happy to be alive. And then you must ask Him for whatever you believe to be a better occupation.

You must be clear in your mind about exactly what you want to do instead of what you find yourself engaged in at the time. I have to reiterate that you must be realistic about your capabilities in this regard, in the sense that you shouldn't choose work that you are not well suited for. It must at least something that you like and are capable of learning to do well. In other words you have to be capable of acquiring the skill set required to do the work.

You are the best placed person to know what you are capable of doing and what you are capable of learning. You have to do your research beforehand into the inherent requirements of the work you now want to do versus your true potential. For instance you shouldn't opt for a career in financial accounting if you're not a numbers person, or for woodwork if you are not a person who enjoys working with their hands.

You have to be mindful of the fact that a career is something that is for the long term and therefore be very careful about the choice you make. You have to ask yourself "Will I be happy doing this for the rest of my life?" "Will I be happy with the type of income that I will derive from the trade ?" You have to make a thorough introspection before you make your final choice.

I know that in my life I have made a few career changes and with each change had a more enjoyable experience. My first real career was as a Quality control officer at a ceiling and partition manufacturing company and that was for me the most boring job I have had in my life. The pay was equally bad. I lived from hand to mouth as a Quality control officer. Even some people who did menial labour earned more than I did. I tried my best everyday but I just didn't have the love for the job because it was something that just landed on my lap. It wasn't something that I chose for myself.

My employer had conducted an aptitude teat on all its employees and thereafter decided that based on my personal results I was well suited for this kind of work. And then I was promoted to the position, without any corresponding change in my wage I must add.

All that was happening in my life then was happening because I had not yet known my true worth. Others decided what was to be good for me and how much they would pay me for that. I was completely at the mercy of the world and I can tell you that that is no way to live.

I only started to do work that I enjoyed for wages that was satisfactory to me when I did work in an occupation that I chose for myself. Some time in the year 1992 I decided that I wanted to be a Traffic Officer. I had a vague idea of what the job requirements were, which was not the ideal situation but I felt that I could make the grade in that field if I were to be given a chance.

I knew that there was a college that offered a three year diploma in Traffic Management and in 1993 I enrolled for the course at that college. I must say those three years were some of the most enjoyable in my life and in the end I obtained the diploma. In the meantime I had obtained a driving license and by the end of the third year I was optimally positioned to land a job in the Traffic profession, which I did in 1997.

I was to go on to work for 15 years as a Traffic Officer. It was a tough job wroth with many changes but as a person who thrives in a challenging environment I had a good time working there. I had the job satisfaction in knowing that I was doing very important work saving lives and changing public road behavior to make the roads in my country to be the safest to drive, cycle, walk and run on.

After Traffic I worked for a Municipal Workers Trade Union as a Regional Secretary and Full-time Shop-steward and I derived even more joy from my work in knowing that I was contributing to harmonious labour relations, educating people in labour laws and human resource policies. I was a leader in a great trade union and I learned so much about myself and so much about what it means to lead people.

I went on to become a Labour Relations Advisor with a different employer and that career I enjoyed also. With all the challenges and difficult situations you have to deal with in the job it was most satisfying because it made me mentally stronger and more resilient in my approach.

I am not talking about these things to boast or anything like that, I am only trying to illustrate the possibility of making a career change for the better by making myself an example. I am a person who subscribes to the notion that variety is the spice of life. Some people would take it further and say a change is as good as a holiday.

Now I know that everyone is different and have their own preferences and standards. I am for this reason not implying that everyone must follow my lead and occasionally change jobs or whatever occupations that they may be engaged in. If you are happy where you are, doing what you are doing then fine, by all means, stay there, but if you hate that place, that environment or those people then you may want to take what I am saying into consideration and make that change. It could mean the difference between life and death for you. Emotional stress can kill you.

The other thing that I have learned about knowing your real worth is that the knowledge gives you the advantage of negotiating from a position of strength. No one can exploit you financially when you know the value of what you are bringing to the table, when you know what value your skills and expertise add to the product or service. Then you are able to tell people to take it or leave it when you have set your price. When you know your true worth you can afford to be choosy in terms of who you offer your services to as a client or employer. You do work for people only when the price is right because you know what the right price is.

I know that I have said in the other books that you are worth a lot for just being a child of God. I have said that you are an heir to an estate that is abundant with everything you need to live an amazing, enjoyable life. I wish I could say that that is all you need to be but I can't because there is no automatic way to make your position as heir to the kingdom of God work for you that does not require any sacrifice and input from you. You have to identify the resources you need to take your life to a higher level and then make good use of them.

And while you are at it remember that the skills and expertise that you now possess you can use to reach for something that you will love more. I am emphasizing the love aspect because I know that you do more, faster and smarter when you are doing something that you love. You can work all day and all night without tiring when you do something that you love. Work doesn't even feel like work when you do something that you love at your workplace. You can't wait for the sun to come out, you can't wait for the day to begin and you are always looking forward to doing all the exciting things that make up your work.

If you haven't found work that you love doing yet or if you are in one that you don't even like, remember that the resources that you can use to get what you want are limitless. You only need to pray to God for Him to reveal them to you, when you have identified them, take action and use them to advance to the answer to your prayer. You don't even have to stop working at your current job to make a change. You can, when you have found something that you think you will love doing, enroll for a course you can study part-time at a college or university.

I know that some might say that tertiary education is not for everyone or that not all of us have the intellectual ability to study further than high school. I know that some might say that when you are working a full-time job you don't have enough time to study and so on and so forth, but all these arguments are but excuses that we make to justify our reluctance or refusal to take action on a thought or idea that could be potentially life changing for us. The real reasons could be laziness, a low self-esteem, a negative self-image or a sheer lack of confidence. I have elucidated on how to deal with these enemies of progress in previous books in the series.

The thief of time for most people I know is the television. Many people spend most if not all their leisure time away from work engaged in one activity, watching television. In most households the television is always on when people are awake. The only time it is switched off is when everyone is asleep because when people are not at school or work, there seems to be an unwritten rule that they must of necessity watch television.

And the television programming is always about stuff that does not take anyone forward. A lot of senseless things are being daily flighted that are actually the garbage that you daily feed your mind.

Well guess what, you could start there to free up the time you need to study for your dream career. Television watching can develop into a habit and I know that a habit can pretend to be an indispensable principle. Unfortunately for TV lovers, that is the sacrifice you have to learn to make. You have to choose between a better future and a happy life on the one hand and forever watching television on the other. With some people it all boils down to just that. So the choice is yours. I am only shining light on some facts.

Whatever you area of expertise or field of endeavor and however good you may be in that area or field, there is always room for improvement. There is always the need to be abreast of prevailing trends and to be ahead of everyone else in your area of expertise to be the preferred contractor, to be the preferred employee. This always comes with financial benefits and that feeling of self confidence and a higher self esteem plus a positive self-image. Sometimes to achieve this you don't have to go and enroll at a college or university.

Sometimes to learn new ways of doing things and improving your skills or adding new ones to the set you already have, you may need only informal education. You can buy books about your vocation or find free online courses on the finer details of your work. You can attend webinars hosted by leaders in your industry. I have learned personally in my life to appreciate the value of informal education. There is so much that I have learned from informal education that I do not believe that you can find in any curriculum in formal institutions of education.

And in informal education the people who deliver the lectures and education are mainly the people who teach what they actually do as experts in their respective fields, as opposed to people who have only read some books in preparation for teaching others.

Informal education can help you add value to your product and services. It can result in noticeable changes to your work and what you bring to the table. It can put you in a position where you are able to negotiate for better remuneration for your services with your employer. It can help you justify charging more for your services as a contractor. Whatever your chosen field of endeavor, in order to be the best and earn more, you have to strive to improve yourself on a continuous basis. I know that I learned to trade stocks in the stock exchanges of the world online. That is what informal education can do for you. You can learn from it stuff you won't find in any curriculum of formal educational institutions.

The resources that you have to use are numberless and available to you if only you effect the interaction between your conscious and Subconscious minds in a deliberate, optimum way, as elucidated in the books before this one in the series. We, as humans have been equipped with the ability to make resources available when we decide to move in a certain direction. We have also been equipped with the knowhow to use those resources to get whatever we want or to become whatever we want to become. There is therefore no justification for people failing to find profitable work that they can do and actually enjoy doing.

Nothing in life beats knowing what you are really worth. Besides it being a safeguard against financial exploitation, the knowledge gives you the freedom to become you in any given circumstance. When you know what you are worth you can dictate terms and have a lot of say in doing what you do. When you know your worth you have choices. You are not stuck anywhere and you can move freely within your chosen field of expertise. There can even be competition for your services.

As I close this chapter I have to bring this important fact to your attention and it is that the change in working environments I dedicated the better part of this chapter to can only be smooth and less demanding if you move within related fields. For instance since my traffic law enforcement days I have moved consistently to another field where I would work with the interpretation and application of the law.

As a full-time shopsteward I interpreted and applied labour laws. As a student of law at university I studied law and graduated as a lawyer. As an Industrial Relations Advisor I interpreted and applied Labour Law. Every field that I have ventured into had something to do with the law. I am not saying that this is the rule of thumb, I am only saying that the approach makes for easy and smooth transition and transformation. As to what would work for you, it is your call.

Chapter 4
Be an optimist

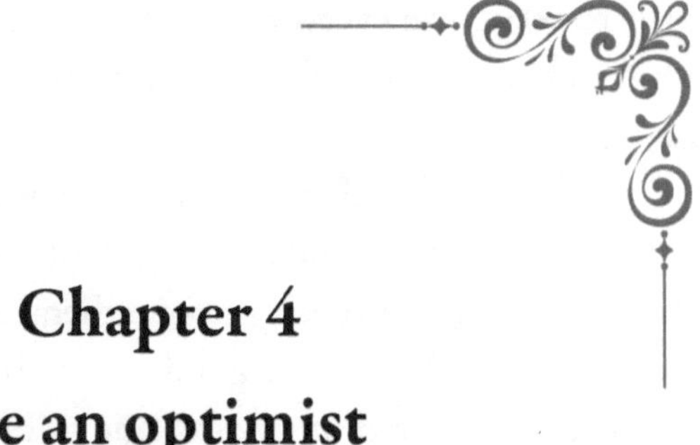

When you listen to, read the news or watch it on television you are guaranteed to learn that there has been so many bad things that have happened recently. The news, regardless of the media where you find it is a compilation of reports about bad things that have happened, are busy happening or are about to happen in the world. And whatever your media of preference, there is no escaping the news and they affect different people differently depending on the level of exposure and maturity of the individual consumer. Our movies and dramas are mostly also about bad things happening in the world and the overall picture that the news junkie and television addict has of the world is one of a terrible place.

Some people in the world are scared into paralysis by what they see and hear in the media. It is very easy to give in to the narrative and conclude that this is the most terrible place anyone can find themselves in, as if we even have an alternative.

It is very easy to be depressed by the things that newsrooms focus their attention on. Some people would go to the extent of giving up on life because of the constant bombardment with bad news that they allow themselves to be subjected to. I guess we have to recognize everyone's right to know about whatever they want to know about, whether it is good for them or not, we have no right to judge

But the truth is that there are only pockets of bad things that happen in the world and it is the job of some people to highlight them and compile reports about them to give an illusion of a world without hope. The good that is happening in the world hardly gets reported on and no one in Hollywood ever makes a movie about the good that people do in the world.

The point that I am trying to make is that in this world that we are living in, it is easy for one to become a pessimist. It is easy to lose hope and give up on your dreams. It is easy to resign oneself to a dreary type of existence wherein there is not much good to look forward to. In other words it is easy to become a negative person. It is a world in which people live in utter despair because of the newsroom and Hollywood narrative.

This state of affairs makes optimists an exception to the rule. Optimists live in the same world as everyone else. This same one that makes some wish they were never born. This type of people believes that the world is better than it used to be and it has the potential to become even better than it is right now. They believe that they have the right to be here and they believe that they are here to do their part in making this a wonderful world for everyone to live in. They believe that as far as the world is concerned, the best is yet to come.

I don't believe that there is a group of people who are especially wired to be optimists. I do believe howeve,r that becoming an optimist or not becoming one is a matter of personal choice. It depends largely on what you are focusing your attention on as an individual, the bad that is happening in the world or the good that is happening here.

The misery that defines some people's lives is in many instances self imposed. I have written in another book of the series that nothing exists in your life save that you are aware of it. Likewise nothing can have any influence on you save when you place your attention on it.

If you want to live a life of success and happiness you have to be very selective in what you focus your attention on. You bring a thing into your life by giving it attention. In this same world there are all kinds of exceptional sports people, all kinds of successful entrepreneurs, all kinds of influential motivational speakers, all kinds of life coaches and a lot of people succeeding in their various fields of endeavor. In this same world there are boundless opportunities for anyone who wants to change their lives for the better. People everywhere get promoted in their jobs everyday. People start their own businesses and generate great wealth for themselves every day.

The above are some of the things that make this a truly wonderful world. You can choose to focus your attention on these and other good and progressive things in life to get motivated to do some good yourself. When you focus on what is good about life you allow yourself to desire growth and pleasurable experiences that personal growth brings with it. You allow yourself to desire the good life for yourself and we know that desire is the springboard of action. Before long you will be looking to see what you need to do to get the nice life.

Pray about it and be very specific about what you desire to have or become. Then will yourself to believe that your possession of the desired thing or your becoming what you intend to become is a as good as done. Rising to this mental state will give you the confidence and courage you need to take the steps necessary to take you closer to the actual fulfillment of your desire.

Enjoy the feeling that you get from seeing yourself in your mind's eye as already having realized your goal and keep visualizing this every chance you get, up to the point where it assumes a definite naturalness about it. This is a sure case way of impressing your Subconscious with your desire in the sense of it being assumed to be an accomplished fact already. This will bring the law of reversibility into play and the Subconscious will make all the resources that you need for the fulfillment of your desire available to you.

No matter how bad things might get in life, the optimist always believes that the best is yet to come and looks forward to a brighter tomorrow, always. This attitude will always stand the optimist in good stead as life is never without challenges, and we need to overcome them in order to succeed and be happy. It is easier to overcome challenges when you believe that you are capable of doing so. Optimists, because of the belief that they have in their capabilities, are almost always confident in their approach to life's problems. Being an optimist definitely gives one an edge in life. An optimist would rather try and fail than fail to try.

The other thing is everyone fails at something at some stage in life. That is a fact of life. So we're all guaranteed to meet with failure at one point or another in our lives. The optimists of the world do get confronted with failure in their lives too. The difference is that when they fail they don't give up.

They review the performance and positively look for positives and possible take aways that they will have to inculcate in their next performance. In other words they look for what went wrong and brainstorm what needs to be done to improve the performance. It is a fact of life that success is not always instantaneous, and it is mostly achieved after one or more failed attempts.

To an optimist there is no failure but lessons learned. Many people who have a full-time occupation and study part-time do not have a smooth ride in that their journey is punctuated with some failed modules along the way. I am still to hear of a professional sports person or team that wins all their games all the time. En route to becoming world beaters they go through some devastating defeats but failure only serves to fire optimists up for a better next performance.

So choose to be an optimist and look forward to the future with anticipation of only good things coming your way. This kind of attitude will unlock the resources you need to succeed and make them available to you. Expect nothing but the very best for yourself.

Chapter 5
Stop being envious

Envy is one of those destructive emotions that many people are vulnerable to. It is not easy to suppress and certainly not easy to manage without serious effort on the envious person's part. I am using the word manage deliberately because I don't believe that it is possible for anyone to be completely devoid of envy.

We all wish we were that Man United striker that has all the dribbling skills and bangs in the winning goals. That is a form of envy. We all wish that we were the ones who wrote and sang that chart busting tune. That's a form of envy. When someone covets what belongs to another because they wish they were the ones owning that particular article or attribute, they are possessed by envy.

Now the problem is that an envious person can move beyond just wishing that they were the one having the attributes or advantages possessed by the target off their envy. Envy gives birth to resentment of the person who is envied, and the envious person can go out of their way to try and destroy that article which is the cause of their envy. They may maliciously damage the article. Sometimes envy causes a person to be murderous and this feeling does get acted upon in some cases.

The truth is that envy, jealousy and hate, among other destructive tendencies,are inherent and inborn in human beings. A casual observation of toddlers will confirm this. They come naturally to us in our infancy and childhood. Children are not at the stage of maturity where they know from experience just how badly these tendencies can harm those that are prone to possessing them. Envy and related emotions can have a suicidal effect on the person they control, in that it can get them to act without thinking at times and it can make them to act irrationally.

Envy has led to the ruin of many promising lives because people tend to pay it too much attention. At whatever stage that you may be in life, there is always going to be people who have more stuff than you have and people who are better at things than you are, inversely, there is always going to be people who have less material things than you have and who are less proficient than you in doing some things. So that makes envy a nonsensical thing to allow yourself to be controlled by. You are never going to be above everyone in everything, ever.

It is easy to deal with envy and eliminate it as a factor in your life if you take into consideration the fact that God gives us all, without discrimination, the same number of hours in a day. Twenty four is all that we all get so no one is getting any unfair advantages where that resource is concerned. The same goes for every other resource. Whatever it may be that you want to have or become, all that we have to do is make use of the unlimited resources at your disposal.

There is no shortage of or disproportionate allocation of resources. Everyone has equal access to the resources we need to get what we want or to become whatever we want to become. We just have to take cognizance of this fact to avoid being envious of other people.

If it is a certain skill that you require to acquire what you desire or to become the person you dreame of becoming, do your research and find the resources that you need to acquire what you desire or to become the person you dream of becoming.

When you desire that outcome so badly that you continually fantasize about already having realized it, the feelings commensurate with your fantasy will make an impression on the Subconscious and it will immediately begin to work on making the resources necessary for its realization available to you. There is no resource beyond its reach.

There is a song by the late Peter Tosh that comes to mind amid this discussion. It is titled "I'm the toughest " and it goes like: "Anything you can do, I can do it better. I'm the toughest." to quote but two sentences. Now that is the kind of attitude that you should adopt towards people whose deeds make you feel envy. You should see yourself as capable of rising to their level and even outperforming them.

This kind of attitude towards envy will make it work for you in that other people's achievements would serve as an inspiration and motivation for you to do better than them, that is if you have any ambitions in that particular field of endeavor.

Envy can easily be managed in this way and a creative outlet can be found for it. Anyway I must mention here that constantly comparing yourself with others is not a healthy way to live. I believe that by wanting to compete with everyone you are putting yourself under undue pressure, staying in your lane and working only on improving yourself and focusing on becoming a better at what you do than you were yesterday is the better option. Exceptional performances by others should only serve as inspiration and motivation provided you are labouring in the same field.

You can avoid unnecessary stress and depression by recognizing the fact that there has never been a person alive who was the best in every aspect of life. This way you will relieve yourself of the pressure that comes with wanting to be number one in everything. We all have our strengths and weaknesses. Choose one area that you want to specialize in and stick to that until your goal is achieved.

People who envy others are generally people who have a low opinion of themselves, people who do not see themselves as capable of achieving feats that those they are envying achieve.

That is mainly because they are not aware of the unlimited resources available in the world for them to use to reach their goals. Whatever anyone can do, we can do ourselves because the same resources that they used to do what they did are available to us as well. Sometimes all you need to do is bring your mind and body. We have plenty of free online courses, free webinars and YouTube videos about everything under the sun so a lack of funds is not a factor anymore in this age of information.

So that in effect renders it intellectual laziness to engage in envious conduct against anyone for any reason. All you need do is look around, as far as the eye can see, there are resources waiting to be taken advantage of. I have two resources in particular that I use every day in pursuit of my goals. They are my android phone and my laptop. I use the phone to write books, design book covers, browse the internet for opportunities, read and send emails, find and apply for jobs online and to do so much more. I use the laptop to store my books and to format and publish them and have them on sale at online and physical bookstores the world over. I own a website where I host a blog that I created on my laptop.

I have not always had these gadgets. They were made available to me by my Subconscious mind when I decided that I wanted to be a writer of books. I have since been able to purchase a course to learn more about my chosen vocation. I have been able to purchase software to make life as an author easier.

I wouldn't have known about some of these resources if I had not seen myself in my mind's eye as a fully fledged writer of books. From that point onwards I didn't have to move a finger in search of resources, they just found me wherever I went. Sometimes all I have to do is open my email and there they will be. I pick and choose which ones I want to use if any at all, I'm comfortable in the knowledge that they are there for me to find and use as I wish. I know that I will never run short of resources to make a success of myself in my line of work.

So I don't need to envy anyone. You can do the same if you are a person who has discovered that pleasure in running your own race. Learning to be happy for others when they achieve their goals and celebrating their success with them gets you in close proximity with success and makes you attractive to success yourself. It is not an easy tendency to develop but as it is with everything else in life, practice makes perfect. When you eventually get the hang of it, celebrating the achievements of others can become second nature to you. Celebration grows accustomed to you too and your Subconscious will create situations in your life to justify a celebration of your own successes.

Envy is a childish emotion and it is one of those things that we have to shed along the way as we grow older and wiser. When you get envious you are giving your Subconscious the impression that you are inadequate, that you are unable to achieve what others achieve, and the Subconscious will work on making the impression that you make on it a reality. You will never find the resources that you need to realize your goals not because they are not there but because you will not be vigilantly on the lookout for them as your focus would be on the abilities and luck of others. What you are not aware of does not exist to you.

No one can ever be able to block the success of people that they don't like or who they feel shouldn't be successful. So for a person who spends their time comparing themselves with others and feeling that they don't measure up, life is most likely stagnant. The resultant emotional stress is likely to cause mental and physical illness. This is a sure case way to disempower yourself because when you are done expending your energy on stressing about other people's success, you will have none left to channel into achieving your own success.

Most likely you will be starting to hatch plots about stopping other people's success. Envy invariably turns people into monsters if not handled correctly. People have succeeded in whatever it is that they wanted to do, it is okay, take that and turn it into an inspiration to set your own goals and pursue them to the best of your ability to achieve your own success. Being envious just dissipates the energy you need to pursue your own goals.

If you let envy rule your life, gradually you will become more and more evil as your envious thoughts take control of your mind. People just don't wake up one day and suddenly become murderers, arsonists and fraudsters. The ideas to commit these crimes come to them through consistency in thinking hateful thoughts that eventually gain control of their minds. It would be just a matter of time before they get the urge to act on the evil ideas that would have taken root in their minds in time.

And then tragedy would result and lives would be destroyed, including that of the person who allowed themselves to be ruled by envy. So you have to learn to deal constructively with envy. Just don't pay it too much attention. Only your focused attention can give life to envy to a point where you lose control of your mind and emotions.

Learning to stay in your lane and minding your own business is the best thing you can do for yourself. The people who find enough energy in their lives to channel into succeeding in their various endeavors are able to do so because they are focused on their own business. They are not always looking over their shoulder to see what the other guys are doing. Remember that your happiness comes from within and that it is only an illusion that anything outside of yourself can make you happy. Happiness is after all only a state of mind that can be attained by looking within yourself.

Chapter 5
Be adventurous

Someone once said that anyone who has never failed in life has never done anything for the first time. There are times in our lives when what we want to do we have never done before and we do not have a living experience of it. We have had to do things for which we have no reference in our experience. And it is okay in such instances, I must hasten to mention, to be tense and a bit frightened, those are the emotions to naturally experience when you are on the verge of becoming great.

It is normal to be tense and uptight as you go about availing yourself to your unfamiliar task. Your belief in yourself and what you are capable of doing will go a long way towards relieving you of the tension and stage fright. First you have to refrain from making a huge announcement when you are about to tackle something that you have never tried your hand at before, just to give yourself space to breathe when you take those first baby steps. This way you don't have to have societal pressures and expectations to deal with in addition to your tasks in initiating the process of moving towards the attainment of your goal. The fewer the people who know about your new venture, the better. That will take care of stage fright to some extent.

I have learned from personal experience that the amount of stage fright one has is always directly proportional to the number of people watching. The larger the audience, the greater the stage fright. And sometimes stage fright can be a cause of distraction and hence can collapse the whole performance when it overwhelms you.

It can cause you to make one misstep from which you might fail to recove,r therefore marring the rest of the performance. .For these reasons big announcements are a no no for me. It pays to keep your adventures to yourself until you reach a point where you can no longer keep them secret because by then you will have the momentum and inertia going for you already. You will have dealt with the initial tension and fright with relative ease.

Being adventurous means being curious about everything and not being afraid of trying things most people would shy away from. I don't know if I am an adrenaline junkie but I am that kind of person who relishes the doing of what people think can't be done. I am an adventurous person like that, I am the guy that wants to show others that it can be done and I have succeeded quite a number of times.

Please let me be understood, I am by no means suggesting that people must be reckless with their lives and take irresponsible decisions. I believe that everyone has a general idea of what they are capable of doing and what would be a bridge too far for them, so let us leave engineering and physical science to those well positioned to tackle them. I'm merely saying that in our quest to be adventurous we shouldn't allow ourselves to be tempted to bite off more than we can chew. We all have an idea of what our strengths and weaknesses are.

Being adventurous goes hand in hand with being courageous. Courage is a mark of a true winner. It takes courage to venture outside of your comfort zone to try your hand at something you know almost nothing about. When I started writing I didn't know anything about it apart from that I could write a few pages on a given topic. That did not deter me at all as I found myself learning everything else as I got along. Look at me now!

When I decided that I want to enroll for a Traffic Management three year diploma I hadn't the slightest idea what Traffic officers do on a daily. I just knew that that was what I wanted for myself and the rest, as they say, is history.

Which brings me to my next point and it is that sometimes we tend to overthink things and that is mainly because of fear coupled with doubt, self-doubt to be precise. Over analysis of the facts where you had decided to venture into something new often results in self-doubt paralyzing the analyst and putting to bed any hopes succeeding in the new venture. The operative phrase in the unending analysis would invariably be "what if?"

Once you have made your decision you have to strike the hammer while the iron is hot. Don't give yourself a lot of time to be asking questions about the adventure before you. Most of the questions will be answered after you've taken the first steps. In the words of Martin Luther Junior: "You don't have to see the whole staircase, just take the first step." That first step will mean that you are taking action already and that first step will tell you what the second step should be and so on and so forth. Nelson Mandela once said: " It always seems impossible till it's done. "

There are in life those things that you will find easy to do, things in which you can succeed at first attempt without any retakes whatsoever, and they are good for boosting your confidence. But there are those which you fail at in spite of bringing your A game. Those are the things that test you character. In those instances you need to be courageous. You need courage to face the naysayers and the doubting Thomases. You need courage to dust yourself up and start all over again.

It takes courage to ask for a rematch with your nemesis, to want to duck into the ring again with the man/woman that whipped you before. The key is to always review the performance and analyze it to see where you got it wrong and how you can improve. You go over the situation to see what went wrong and what corrections can be made, and what lessons can be learned from it. Once you have collected all the data it will tell you how to approach the next attempt. That is how to garner the courage required, that and the belief that the best is yet to come.

In some endeavors you have to be prepared to be in it for the long haul. Some things need thorough preparation for one to succeed in. In some fields it is the level of preparedness that determines whether you win or lose. You must spare no effort in this regard. You have to make optimum use of the resources at your disposal to ensure that you are well prepared. If it's online courses that you need, spare no expense, if you need to watch training videos, make the time and concentrate, if it's webinars you must attend, by all means do so.

Just remember that the resources that you need to do what you want to do or to become what you want to become are in existence and they are limitless. You will have to be an optimist in order to identify them and put them to good use. Remember also that courage is not absence of fear, it is when we act in spite of our fear that we act courageously. The fear we can also minimize by being thorough in our planning and preparation. This way we can minimize the chances of failure so we can get in there high in confidence. That on its own increases our chances of success.

So acting with courage could be as a result of having taken proper care of the preliminaries. You therefore have to do all that is necessary to give yourself an advantage. And sometimes you need to be doing something that you really love to be able to prepare well.

Courage is easy to muster when you are in love with what you are doing. Which makes it important to choose something that you love when choosing a career. It is that love that gives you the courage to continue even when the chips are down and the going is tough.

Chapter 6
Stop living to impress other people

Now everyone of us would very much like to have people think highly of us all the time. Most people rate very highly what people think of them, they are overly preoccupied with how they look in the eyes of their fellow men. Some would place a lower value on how they look to themselves. The impression we make on others can become an all-consuming preoccupation with some of us.

Making a good impression on people is not necessarily a bad thing, it only becomes a problem when it is an overriding preoccupation. Then people can easily resort to some unorthodox methods to obtain a validation from others. Incurring unnecessary debt to purchase luxury items that we cannot afford is one of the ways we try to get people to respect us. We go out and buy expensive cars and clothes on credit to give people an impression that we are wealthy.

Now I am one of those people who believe that good personal finance requires that you live within your means and put away ten percent of your monthly income to pay yourself. I also believe in delaying gratification if we can't afford what we desire currently. We have to find ways that would make acquisition of the things that we desire easier and more convenient.

We could make time to learn how to invest in the stock market and use our savings in that regard. Or we could move into a more lucrative career from which we would derive more income so we can buy the nice things without strangulating ourselves with bad debt.

Now don't get me wrong, I'm not for people denying themselves things that they want because I'm against people getting themselves nice things. No. Not at all. I'm against the practice of buying luxury items on credit to impress other people or to show them that you are wealthy enough to afford those things when you know that you are not.

Trying to keep up with the Joneses can be such a cruel trap for the gullible to fall into. Let's face it, no one but the Joneses know how they are able to afford those big expensive cars and the double storey house. How they are able to take their children to the most expensive schools only the Joneses know. There is no wisdom in competing with them because you don't know what resources they have access to that enable them to live this large. They could have won the lottery or they might have cashed in on some life insurance. There are just a lot of possibilities where the source of their wealth is concerned.

Many folks have learned the hard way that it is unwise to compete with the Joneses. Imagine losing your job while you are still paying off your mortgage loans and car and furniture installments. That is the time when it dawns on many people that they own less than nothing.

Imagine the emotional trauma of being evicted from that house you've been calling your house for many years. Imagine them coming to repossess your car and furniture. Overnight you could end up with less than nothing, from appearing to have everything.

Imagine the eventual shame of being handed over to the credit bureau and being declared not creditworthy. Imagine the pain of seeing your children being kicked out of the high fee schools. Imagine the strain that all of this would have on the marriage. Is it worth putting on that façade of wealth and living large for a while?

I have said it before and I will say it again, try as much as it is possible to live within your means. Stay in your lane and mind your own business. The only person you should be competing with is yourself. Try whatever you can to improve yourself from what you've been to what you can be.

Delay gratification while you make plans to make acquisition of luxury items that you want easy. Never purchase on credit things you can have for cash with a little delay in gratification. Sometimes all you need do is exercise some restraint and patience to save you years of misery.

You don't need anyone to validate you and you certainly don't want to act to your detriment only for acceptance by the folks in your hood. Dare to be different and set standards for yourself that you can attain and sustain. Do not punch above your weight. Living beyond your means is a risky kind of lifestyle and your bubble can burst anytime for any number of reasons.

Learn to live to invest your time and money instead of spending them. Spending time is more like watching television for hours on end just because it is switched on and you're watching whatever is on at the time. Investing your time is like reading that book to learn a new skill. Watching that YouTube training videos to sharpen and hone your skills. It is tuning in to that webinar to learn new ways of doing things.

Spending money is more like using your hard earned cash to buy luxury items that do not earn you money in any way. Investing money is more like paying for resources and tools you need to make you more proficient in your line of work. Optimum use of those tools and resources should make it easy to make more money in your chosen profession.

For a writer the tools and resources would be gadgets like a smart or Android phone, a laptop and some software. For a stock market trader the tools and resources would be a phone and laptop as well, and trading software like an online trading platform and some charting services platforms if you're a technical analyst.

Make progressive use of your money. The ten percent that I told you to pay yourself from your monthly income you should put aside, not for a rainy day. Saving for a rainy day attracts the rainy day and all that the money can be used for is the rainy day when, not if it comes.

Rather put away the money to invest in worthy ventures that are sure to come up in the future. You must put it away so that when an investment opportunity comes up it should find you ready. So that when the time comes to make purchases of luxury items the profits from your investments pay for them and not your hard earned money.

This is how other people will be impressed, with a wealth that is not fake. That is how you will be able to have a standard of living that you can attain and maintain without breaking the bank. This is how you will know that self-validation is all the validation you need.

Get everyone in your household to adopt the culture of investing rather than one of spending. This could turn out to be the decisive factor in the creation of transgenerational wealth with everyone playing a part. You can be as deliberate as all that in generating real wealth instead of creating a fake fragile one for the reason of impressing other people. Staying in your lane and minding your own business is a good starting point.

Chapter 7

Learn to manage your resources well.

I am writing this chapter assuming that the reader is in possession of some resources including but not limited to some property or some personal items, for example gadgets like a cell phone and laptop and maybe some cash also. I know that some people are earning some money from their employment or their businesses, this chapter is written with them in mind also.

Now I choose to look at the world as full of opportunities for those who are in the lookout for them. That is how I choose to look at the world because that view is in line with my beliefs about what is possible for the optimist. People who are on the look out for opportunities generally are in the know about what you need to be able to take advantage of the opportunities when they present themselves. They are usually clear about the requirements to be met for one to be considered for the opportunity.

Now the items I referred to above are resources that if used correctly can help you take advantage of opportunities that may appear on your radar. You have the resources and the ability to add others should your situation so demand, so you should be clear about what you want to achieve. When you pray to God for His help you should be absolutely clear about precisely what it is that you desire to achieve and then be vigilantly expectant about your dream materializing eventually.

You have to look at what you have to see how you can use it to get what you want. In the case of someone looking for employment or someone who is employed and is looking for greener pastures, they must be sure about the type of employment and the kind of work that they are looking for. They must additionally be sure that they meet the requirements of the job and if they don't they must do their research to determine the ways that are available to them to ensure that they meet those requirements.

Employment agencies have online platforms where they advertise vacancies, all that they require for you to use these platforms to apply for jobs you are interested in is that you upload your resume, certificates, diplomas and degrees on their website and you are good to go. With this innovative resource jobs look for you wherever you are and you can apply even on your mobile phone with much ease. It has become that easy to do job seeking when you have the right resources.

Online trading platforms belonging to Stock market brokers bring the stock market trading floor to a trader wherever they are. Trading software is available for those who want the convenience of their use. All that you need as a trader is a laptop or mobile phone and an internet connection and you are good to go. All of the above are resources that are plentiful for you to find and use if you are in that line of work.

For every, and anything that you want to do there are similar resources. To join a webinar you need an email address, a mobile phone or a laptop, a webinar app and an internet connection. Most webinars that I personally have attended were free for subscribers of the product or service of the person organizing the webinar. In order for you to obtain advice on the possibilities and opportunities in whatever field of endeavor, in a webinar, the above resources are indispensable.

It has almost become compulsory in today's world for everyone to possess a mobile phone, a laptop and an email address. And then there are apps that you have to download to your gadgets for every online activity. For online meetings you have your Zoom and Skype. These are all resources that are an absolute requirement for anyone that wants to transform their lives for the better in the world of today. Anyone with big dreams would do well to invest their money in these resources, which generally make life easier when used correctly.

I know that you can't do much as a new Indie author without prior experience or as an aspiring author, without some of these gadgets and applications, you need the relevant resources to help you get acquainted with the tools of your chosen trade. I'm talking about writing courses, book marketing and promotion websites, SEO tools for keywords and category research etcetera etcetera. The world has become very small and you will find that everything you need to succeed in today's world is virtually at your fingertips.

You may be the entrepreneur type with ideas that you believe can make a difference in your and fellow human beings' lives but lack the start up capital. Then applying for a loan could be the way to go for you. That is if you are unable to convince friends and family to invest in your product or idea. That is the only way that you can obtain a good debt.

I call it a good debt because it is a debt obtained in order to make an investment in something that is capable of bringing in returns for the entrepreneur. It is a debt that the business itself can pay off. When you are on the lookout for resources that can take you forward towards the realization of your goal they will appear.

Conclusion

Having come to the end of this fifth and last book in the series I think that it is proper to do one final recap of the various topics discussed in The Undying Faith series. I did write at length about the human mind and tried to elucidate on its tremendous power in making things happen for the individual human being.

I wrote about the two components of the human mind which are the conscious and Subconscious minds and how to deliberately use the natural interplay between them to make realization of your desires a reality. I have explained this interaction from a Biblical perspective. Paul did advise people to think positive thoughts thus prescribing a mental diet of things that are true, honest, pure and of good report among others. He knew that if these were the things that we keep in mind always, the Subconscious mind would out picture them and we would live a life of success and happiness.

What you allow your mind to continually dwell on is the diet that you feed your mind and that will be taken up by the Subconscious and made real in your life. I also touched on the psychology of self-image and how it shapes your personality and makes you what you are. I touched on this very important topic of inner conversations and how decisive they are in fashioning your personal conditions and circumstances.

I wrote about the need to change your inner conversations if you want to change your personal circumstance and conditions. Personal circumstance and conditions, whatever they may be, are merely a reflection of your inner conversations. What you think and believe about yourself, that is what you are, and your conditions and circumstance will take shape in accordance and in harmony with that.

I wrote about the human being's place in the universe and the relationship between God and man. I wrote about what this relationship means in real terms and the humongous power that it affords man. Man is a creator because he has the creative God force in him and recognition of this fact makes man aware of the immense power he wields.

I have written at length about how to pray prayers that yield results and how you must use the faculty of imagination to visualize your fulfilled desire when you pray and why this is necessary. This explanation of the psychology of prayer is necessary for the purpose of demystifying the concept of prayer itself, and for the purpose of shedding light on why the Bible teaches us to pray the way it teaches us to. It should be clear to you now that merely closing your eyes and uttering some words is not all there should be to prayer.

It is important for the concept of prayer to be explained to Christians so that they will learn how to pray properly and not do things they mistakenly believe to be prayer and then become discouraged when they don't receive what they are praying for. I hope that I have been clear enough in my explanation so that you, the reader can put to the test these principles and benefit from this ancient wisdom.

I also wrote about the difficulties brought about by diversity and the need for the individual to dare to be different. In the process of charting your path to success and happiness you will encounter resistance in many guises with people wanting to derail your dreams and bring you down. Everyone has dreams and aspirations but it is not everyone that would take positive action on such dreams and aspirations and you therefore stand out like a sore thumb when you decide to do so. Then you become an easy target for enemies of progress to take pot shots at in trying to bring you down.

That is where the need to be able to assert yourself becomes essential to your success. If you fall at this hurdle you can forget about ever being successful at anything and you most definitely won't be a happy person. No one can really be happy living a lie. Self-assertiveness is an indispensable quality for those who have goals that they want to achieve. Success and happiness are related in that happiness follows success. You get happy when you succeed in something that you love doing. It is important that we learn how to succeed and be happy. I hope that I have shown clearly in this series of books how you can be successful and happy.

From the author

Thank you for taking time out to read this book. That in itself makes the effort put in writing it justified. I have a small favor to ask of you, if you have enjoyed the book, please leave a review on the product page on Amazon. That will be highly appreciated by this newbie author.

Thanks once again, and God bless

Hebert McQuinn.

Don't miss out!

Visit the website below and you can sign up to receive emails whenever Hebert McQuinn publishes a new book. There's no charge and no obligation.

https://books2read.com/r/B-A-ZOHU-RFMAC

BOOKS 2 READ

Connecting independent readers to independent writers.

Also by Hebert McQuinn

The undying faith.

The undying faith BOOK 1. A guide to a life of success and happiness

The undying faith Book 2. A guide to a life of success and happiness

The undying faith Book 3. A guide to a life of success and happiness

The undying faith Book 4. A guide to a life of success and happiness

The Undying Faith Book 5. A Guide to a Life of Success and Happiness

The Undying Faith

The Undying Faith Book 1. A Guide to a Life of Success and Happiness

The Undying Faith Book 2. A Guide to a Life of Success and Happiness

The Undying Faith Book 3. A guide to a Life of Success and Happiness

The Undying Faith Book 4. A Guide to a Life of Success and Happiness

About the Author

Hebert McQuinn is a former Traffic Officer and Peace Officer. After serving fifteen years as Traffic Officer and Peace Officer he was elected to serve for three years as a Rigional Secretary for a Local Government trade union. Whilst working in this capacity as a full-time employee, he went on to study part time and obtain a Law degree. And then, being a keen student of life that he is, he felt inpired to write about the lessons that life has taught him, hoping that his writings woulkd help some reader somewhere in the world. The result of that inspiration is the four part series of which this particular book is the first instalment.